Beginner's Guide to

Traditional Japanese

Embroidery

First published in Great Britain 2001

Search Press Limited
Wellwood, North Farm Road,
Tunbridge Wells, Kent TN2 3DR

ISBN 0 85532 857 6

The Publishers and author can accept no responsibility for any consequences arising from the information, advice or instructions given in this publication.

Suppliers

If you have difficulty in obtaining any of the materials and equipment mentioned in this book, then please visit the Search Press website for details of suppliers: www.searchpress.com

Alternatively, you can write to the Publishers at the address above, for a current list of stockists, which includes firms who operate a mail-order service.

Publishers' note

All the step-by-step photographs in this book feature the author, Julia D. Gray, demonstrating traditional Japanese embroidery. No models have been used.

In memory of Tokinaga-san, my mentor and friend.

Acknowledgements

I would like to say my biggest thank you to both Kurenai-kai (Japan) and the Japanese Embroidery Center (USA) for taking me on the biggest journey of discovery in my life. It is thanks to them and all my teachers that I have begun to achieve my goal in mastering the exquisite art of *shi-shu* – traditional Japanese embroidery. They alone have helped me strive for the perfection I seek in my work. I can think of no better path to follow in my pursuit of *nui-do* – the Way of the Needle – than the one I have taken.

Thanks also to: Yusai Fukuyama for taking the mystery out of Japanese crafts for me; Tokinaga-san for guiding me along the path; Keiko Utsumi for her enthusiasm and encouragement with her *zokka* – the art of flowers; Anna Jackson and all at the V & A Museum for allowing me special study time with their wonderful textiles and artefacts; Akemi Narita, Mary Tamakoshi, Sue Leighton-White and all my friends who have indulged my interests and supplied my needs in their own special ways.

Beginner's Guide to
Traditional Japanese
Embroidery

Julia D. Gray

SEARCH PRESS

Contents

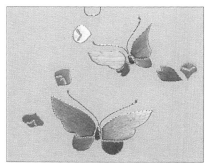

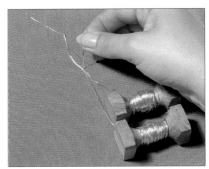

Introduction

For me silk is the only truly scrumptious natural fibre – it has such life and shine. Embroidery on this beautiful fabric has been worked in many countries, but I find the perfection aspired to in traditional Japanese embroidery a wonderful challenge.

Little did I know when I visited the Great Japan exhibition in the 1980s that the kimono displayed there would light a spark inside me and change my life completely, taking me to the far side of the world. I wanted to learn all about the embroidery of a country with over a thousand years of tradition and symbolism. My journey was inspiring and enlightening. I found in traditional Japanese embroidery not just a way to stitch, but also a philosophy that allowed me to achieve balance and harmony in my everyday life.

In Japan, many of the traditional ways of learning cannot be taught. When learning how to embroider, an apprentice must sit in silence and watch the master as he stitches, absorbing his knowledge and skill. To sit and watch a master embroiderer in this way is to be given a great gift in life. You must look carefully and 'steal the knowledge'. If you ask too many questions, this shows that you do not really 'see'. The apprentice observes in this way and practises until his or her work is unrecognisable from that of the master.

I began my adventure into Japanese embroidery in the same way – by copying the work of one far more proficient than I. Designs were devised in phases, allowing me to learn

The kimono has always been designed using panels which are same width as the looms. Two panels make up the back, two panels make up the front, and each sleeve is made with one panel. A little extra silk is used to complete the garment. The sash worn over the kimono – the Obi, is made of a similar width of silk. It is usually a heavier weight as it relies on the stiffness of the fabric to hold its shape. Embroidery on an Obi can be much heavier, as the fabric is able to support thicker threads.

Japanese embroidery was originally designed for kimono, which allowed for the play of light as the wearer moved, so do not view your work from just one position – watch it change with the light. This is the same embroidery lit from different angles.

more techniques with each phase. After completing phase ten, it was considered that I had practised all the basic techniques. I had to show examples of my own stitching to the teacher, illustrating how the technique should look. I discovered that it is impossible to stitch successfully in fine silk if you are unhappy or angry. To stitch, peace must first be attained, then the gentle rhythm of the needle and thread flowing through the silk lowers your rate of breathing as you relax into your work.

This book shows you how to lay flat silk, how to twist your own threads and how to use holding grids. Simple projects will help to develop your techniques, taking their inspiration from the four seasons. Metallic threads can be used to add sparkle to both stitched and couched work, but the shine, shade and life in your embroidery will appear with the way that you stitch, the play of light on the threads and your aim for perfection. Be sparing with your design and embellishment, as less really is more – the eye of the viewer should be allowed to fill in the gaps left - so do not feel you must cover the whole fabric with thread or fill in every space. It is not considered wise or in good taste to dot every 'i' and cross every 't'. The Japanese have a saying: 'Too much done is nothing done'.

So, good luck with this first step on a pathway to untold riches. My only wish now is that I live long enough to achieve my life's ambition – to stitch all that I have in mind!

History

Legend has it that some one thousand years ago, a priest carried a few silk cocoons hidden in his hollow cane out of China. Along with the teachings of his religion he carried the word of sericulture (silk making) to Japan. It is said a Chinese Empress taking tea had dropped a cocoon into her cup and was amazed to see it unravel into a fine thread.

It is more likely that visiting Chinese armies took their culture into Korea and Korean craftsmen carried the Chinese methods of sericulture and silk embroidery into Japan. Whatever the route Buddhism took into Japan – silk embroidery certainly followed.

At first embroideries were only seen in temples and featured the teachings of Buddha. The oldest mention of an embroidered Buddha was in 604 AD but nothing remains of this for students to examine. In 622 AD the oldest remaining example of Japanese embroidery was stitched, and I have been lucky enough to see a reproduction of this piece displayed at the *Chugu-ji* convent in Nara, Japan. It is called *Tenjukoku Mandala*, '*Tenjukoku*' being the Land of Heavenly Longevity where it is believed that people with good karma are invited by Buddha. The convent also owns fragments of the original embroidery, which was commissioned in memory of Prince Shotoku, who had done much to popularise Buddhist worship in his lifetime.

The next step in the evolution of Japanese embroidery came when worshippers wanted their own personal shrines, and embroidered gods appeared in their homes.

An embroidered god. Worship was the earliest use of embroidery in Japan.

In the tenth century – the Heian Period – there was a rigid class structure in Japan, starting with noblemen and warriors and descending to farmers, craftsmen and finally merchants. The need to embellish the dress of high ranking court members, so they could be identified by the colour and decoration of their outfits, moved embroidery into a new field. It became customary for ladies to wear many layers of kimono, each in a different hue, showing in layers at the neck, hem and sleeves. This costume was called *juni-hitoe* or 'twelve-layered dress'.

In *Noh* theatre, the richness, colour and pattern of embroidery began to be used to enhance the atmosphere of a play. As these plays were viewed from a distance, characters were recognised by the designs and colour of their costumes.

The warrior class or *Samurai* were now gaining importance in a political sense, taking the dominance away from court officials. They added their influence to the development of costume, which reflected changes in the social order.

At one time, expensive cloth and embroidery were banned, and at this time it became fashionable to have elaborate linings inside simple outfits.

Finally embroidery reached more of the population. Women passed on their kimono to their daughters. When a daughter was born, her family planted a *paulownia* tree, the wood of which has mothproofing properties.

A traditional Japanese silk weaving loom. The width of these looms still determines the width of fabric used for Japanese embroidery.

The many layers of kimono traditionally worn at court.

On her coming of age the tree was chopped down and a chest was made to house her collection of kimono.

A woman needed at least one kimono for every season. The design of her kimono changed to reflect the stages of her life: sleeves became shorter for a married woman and colours became darker.

Today it is very expensive to own several sumptuous kimono. If your family has not passed down a selection, it is costly to set up your own wardrobe. For this reason, wedding kimono and dress kimono can be hired.

With the passing of the formal dress era, traditional Japanese embroidery must move with the times. Embroidery has long since been found on the screens which divide the Japanese home. Looking to the future, it may be this kind of interior display that keeps this fine craft alive. The evolution continues.

Materials & equipment

Fabric

There are various types of Japanese silk fabrics available, and they are all woven in one width. This is approximately 34cm (13½in) from selvedge to selvedge, which is the same size as the centuries old silk looms.

I use a thick **Habotai** silk for small and finer pieces. **Shioze** is a ridged silk made for Japanese wedding outfits. It gives a firm base for embroidery and can be dyed easily. **Nishijin**, woven in that area of Kyoto, has a lovely texture, and sometimes small motifs are featured in the silk, or gold threads are woven in. **Shusu** is a smooth surfaced fabric which is especially nice in black.

There are other types of silk available which are suitable for Japanese embroidery, but if you are a beginner, I would recommend the above.

Threads

Flat silk threads are used and these are available in hanks or on spools. If you are a beginner, it is advisable to use spools, as the silk strands are wound on to them from the hank without any twist. The silk strands should be worked flat, so taking them from the spool makes stitching easier.

Wooden spools called *koma* are used to hold metallic threads securely during stitching.

Couching threads are made by splitting flat silk threads into finer strands. These are used to couch metallic threads.

From left to right: white and black shioze, *two pink kimono silks, blue and green kimono silks, two patterned white* Nishijin, *bright orange* shusu, *and three antique green silks.*

Threads used for traditional Japanese embroidery. Metallic threads (bottom right) are used on koma (middle right). Half of a skein is wound on to each koma, winding anticlockwise towards yourself in a beckoning motion. Hanks of silk thread are shown at the top, and spools at the bottom.

11

Needles

Handmade needles are always used and they are available in different sizes. This allows the embroiderer to select the correct needle for the thickness of thread being used. The size of the needle should be wide enough to allow the thread to pass through the silk fabric without dragging, but should not be so wide that a visible hole is created. However, note that the steaming and pressing of the finished piece will not only 'set' the silk and lift the shine – it will also close the needle holes, provided they are not visibly too large to begin with.

The right needle size is especially important with flat silk: if the hole is too small, the silk will snag and fray; if it is too big, the flat silk will lie looking like separate strands on the surface, which is not desirable.

A longer, thicker needle is used to lace the silk fabric on the frame.

The needle felt is a work station 'port' at which to place all your needles when you are not stitching. It also protects your needles from loss, damage or rust when they are not in use.

Use an emery strawberry to clean your needles, running the needle through cotton cloth several times before you begin stitching again,  otherwise you will leave a dirty mark in your silk when you next use your needle. This should always be done if your needle begins to squeak as it passes through the silk. It is not considered good etiquette to have a 'singing' needle!

If your needle becomes blunt, or has a small burr on the end (which can happen if you drop your needle on to the floor, point down), then sharpen it by rubbing with very fine sandpaper. This will also clear small spots of rust if you have been careless enough to let your needles get damp.

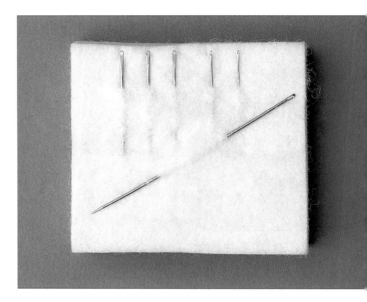

Two machine-made needles, three handmade, one lacing needle, all shown on a needle felt.

Needle guide
Machine-made needles m2 or m3 are used for couching.
Handmade needles:
F5 or F6 for 0.5 flat or 1/1 twist
F7 for 1 flat or 2/1 twist
F8 for 1.5 flat or 3/1 twist
F9 for 2 flat or 4/1 twist

Basic tool kit

Awl The awl acts as a post on which the threads are anchored when they are being cut or twisted. It is also used when tightening the lacing threads.

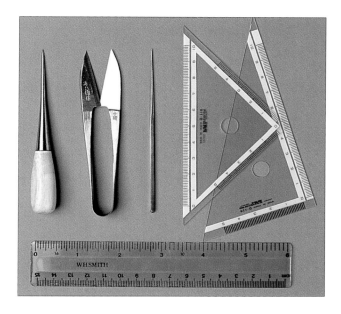

Scissors Scissors should have a smooth finish, with no sharp screw heads, so they do not damage the silk fabric. Traditional Japanese scissors are best, as they have no screw fixing at all, so when fastening off through your completed laid threads, there is no chance of snagging your perfect stitching.

Stroking needle A stroking needle, which is known as a *teko-bari* or *kote-bari*, is used to stroke the silk flat and hold it under pressure until the next stitch is placed.

Set squares and small ruler These are used for the accurate measuring of angles and lines. As they are laid across finished stitching, they should have smooth surfaces.

Transferring equipment

Wooden board This is placed under your silk fabric mounted on your frame, to give a firm base on which to draw your design.

Flat-headed pins These are used instead of round-headed pins, as they cause less marking of the silk.

Chaco paper This is a type of transfer paper, similar to dressmaker's carbon. It does not mark the silk if you happen to rest your hand on an area, and does not smudge. It gives a fine line that can be carefully erased using a slightly damp cotton bud, or left to fade in time. Since lines fade, if the work is to be left for some time before completing, I recommend that major lines be couched or stitched in place as a more permanent guide to where to embroider.

Embossing tool The embossing tool is used to 'draw' over the lines of the design by pressing gently on the chaco paper. If a pencil or pen is used instead, there is always the risk that it will pierce the design paper and transfer paper and make a line on the silk that cannot be erased.

Other items

Frame The traditional frame used in the home, or by the professional embroiderer, is rectangular and made of wood. It is made to accommodate the traditional width of silk fabric, but is available in different lengths. The frame featured here is a regular size.

Magnifying glass An aid to viewing, especially for the finest work.

Cotton ends These are strong, even-weave 100 per cent cotton ends that are stitched to the silk fabric to extend it for securing through the frame's rollers. This allows for the expensive silk fabric to be the right size for the design with no waste.

Sewing machine Used to stitch cotton ends on to the silk, as a firm, stitched line is very important.

Long ruler Used to measure distances when framing up your fabric before embroidering.

Lacing thread I use crochet cotton to lace the silk fabric on to the frame, but any thick, strong cotton thread would be suitable. There is a traditional lacing cotton available.

Chopsticks and wedges Used to secure the frame, after stretching the fabric, before embroidery can begin.

Saw For cutting chopsticks to size.

Cover When you are not stitching, you must always cover the work with acid-free tissue paper and a cloth, to protect it from dust or damage. This cover is also known as a *furoshiki*. These are sold in Japan for carrying shopping, and in other countries as scarves.

Acid-free tissue paper Used to cover your work and protect it from rubbing, dust and light.

Pounding cushion A lint-free silk cushion filled with collected snippings, used to pound the embroidery on the back to release any dust that may have settled in the work and dulled the colours of the silk.

Glue Traditionally, rice paste was used to glue the back of the stitching to anchor it in place, but I use a more modern glue so as not to encourage mould to form when the embroidery is framed. This was not a problem on kimono as the embroidery work was not encapsulated in any way, but free to breathe.

Paint brush A short, chisel-ended paint brush of stiff bristle is best, as it will not flick or splatter the glue, just spread it smoothly. The brush should of course be clean, so as not to spoil the silk thread.

Tray and kettle Used to steam the silk as part of the finishing of the embroidery.

Finishing paper and iron Finishing paper (baking parchment) is much thicker than tissue paper. It is used to protect your stitching from the direct heat of the iron while the embroidery is being pressed.

Card I use museum-quality conservation grade card. This helps to lengthen the life of the embroidery, as it is acid-free, with no chemicals to damage the silk.

Silk wadding I mount my embroidery over silk wadding to give a softer finish to my work.

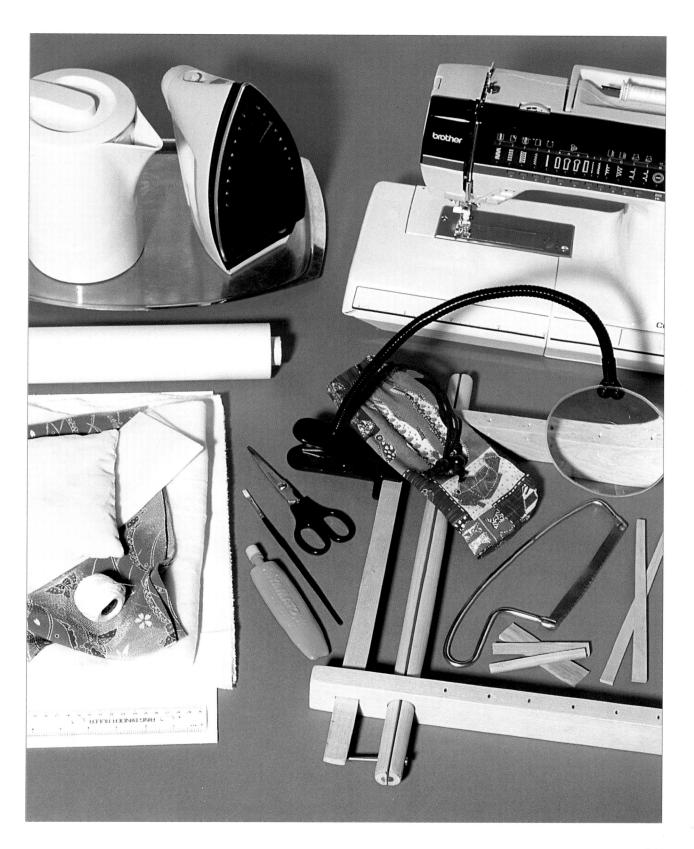

Getting started

The work station

The first thing to remember is: 'tidy work station, tidy mind'. Traditional Japanese embroidery is stitched with the right hand on top and the left hand underneath, so necessary tools are placed to the right, in the waste cotton area.

To set up your work station, you will need daylight coming in from the left-hand side – this means you will not be blocking light with your body or working hand. If you are using a lamp, it should also be a source of light coming from the left. The other working rules to remember are: stitch top to bottom and left to right. This means that your arm or hand will not keep passing over or rubbing a stitched area as you work.

Julia works in the traditional way, sideways on to the design, with her right hand on top and her left hand beneath the fabric. Her Japanese scissors, needle felt, koma and silk thread are neatly placed on the waste cotton at the edge of her embroidery.

16

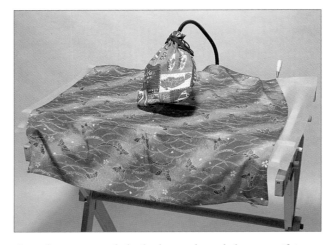

A professional embroiderer in a Kyoto workshop.

Since you work from the side of your embroidery, you need only stretch to the centre of the design, as the other side can be stitched by turning the frame round, or moving to the other side of the frame. The reason for working sideways on to a design stems from tradition: kimono are made up in whole panels, the full length of the garment, so it would be impossible to stitch a design upright. However, each panel is the traditional width of 34cm (13½in), so working from the sides of each panel, the embroidery can be completed with ease. This sideways-on method of working also reduces the danger of spoiling an area you have already stitched.

Always remember to remove your sharp tools, cover your work with acid-free tissue paper and your *furo-shiki*, and also cover your magnifying glass, even if only leaving your work station for a moment, as then there will be no regrets! The sun, in particular, is your enemy, as it will fade your silk, or even burn it with the help of the magnifying glass.

A work station with both the work and the magnifying glass covered to protect the embroidery.

Framing up

Before you begin your embroidery, you need the silk fabric to be centred on your frame, between equal amounts of cotton ends. Once the cotton ends are sewn on and the fabric is placed in the frame, one and a half turns of the roller at both ends should pull the fabric drum-tight. Centring the fabric in this way is very much a matter of trial and error. Try placing the cotton ends in the rollers by eye, then twist the rollers one and a half times to see how taut the silk is. When you think the fabric is placed correctly, follow the procedures in steps 3–7 below.

1. Use a sewing machine to stitch waste cotton fabric to your silk. Make sure the seams are on the top.

2. Place the cotton ends between the rollers, with the seams uppermost.

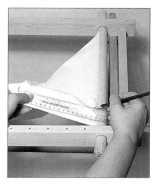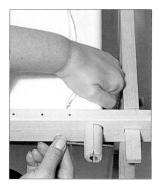

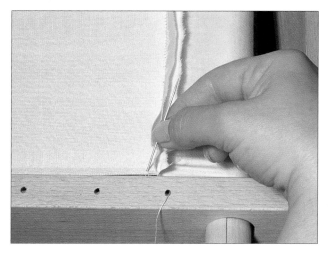

3. Measure from your stitching line with a ruler and make three marks on the cotton ends to keep the silk fabric straight in the frame. The marks should be where the cotton ends will enter the slot of the roller: one mark in the middle and one at each side. One and a half turns of the roller at each end should pull the fabric drum-tight.

4. Twist the rollers to pull the silk drum-tight, and push in the nails. Now lift the frame and push its sides closer to the edges of the silk, ready for lacing.

5. Using a lacing needle and crochet thread, go down through the first hole and come up a third of the way between the first hole and the next, in the selvedge. Do not try to gauge a cut length of thread. Leave the ball of crochet cotton attached until you have stitched to the other end.

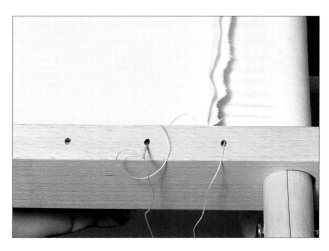

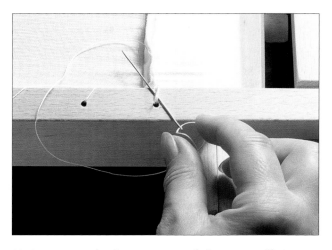

6. Go down a third of the way further along the selvedge. Come up between the silk fabric and the frame. Go down through the second hole of the frame. Continue until you reach the other end.

7. Return to the beginning and, leaving sufficient thread to fasten off at each end, cut your thread from the ball and tie off by taking the thread around the wood three times, then fasten with a buttonhole stitch.

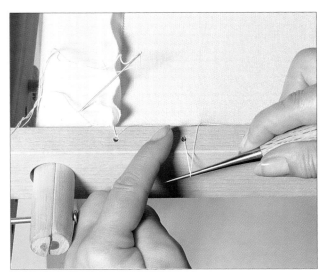

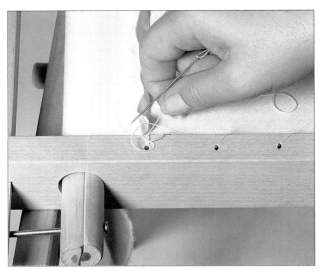

8. Thread a needle at the other end. Pull up the threads all the way along with the awl, three times, until there is no slack in the thread.

9. Fasten off at the end with two or three stitches over the thread to anchor it. Repeat the whole process (steps 5–9) at the other side of the frame.

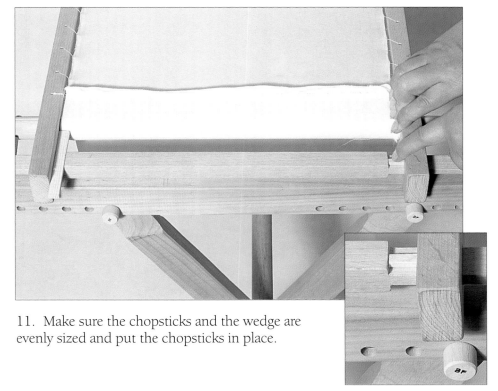

10. The sides of the frame need to be wedged apart to pull the fabric drum-tight width ways. A coin should bounce off it! Put a wedge in the nail side first, and saw chopsticks to size to wedge the other side. Make sure the wedges are the same size on each end to ensure an even stretch.

11. Make sure the chopsticks and the wedge are evenly sized and put the chopsticks in place.

Transferring the design

Designs for Japanese embroidery are 'drawn' on to the silk using chaco paper and an embossing tool. The faint blue lines produced are designed to fade in time, so if you are going to leave your design for some time, stitch around the main lines with couching thread in either the background colour, or the colour you are going to stitch in.

1. Place a hard-covered book or a board, or both, under your framed silk, up to the height of the silk. This is to ensure that, when you draw on the silk, you are not pressing it down. Be careful to use something that will not be marked by your embossing tool.

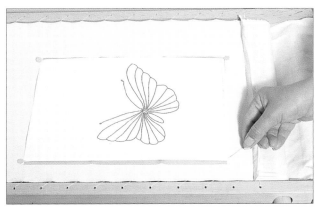

2. Place a sheet of chaco paper, wax side down, on top of the silk, then position your design on top of that, right side up. Pin each corner with the flat-headed pins.

3. Use an embossing tool to trace around the design.

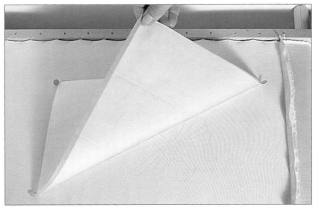

4. Remove the chaco paper and design. If the pins have left marks on the silk, these can be removed using a cotton bud and a tiny spot of clean water.

Choosing colours

Early morning light is the very best light by which to choose your colours. I start the day in the traditional way of the Japanese apprentice, working in the garden and feeding the animals. By then my eyes are attuned to the colours of nature and I feel ready to select the colours for my next project. If you don't have good light from a window in your house, do not be afraid to take your silks outside to choose. Look at the range of colours on the fabric and then stand back to look at your choice. If you want an objective view, look at the colours in a mirror. You will then see if a particular colour stands out as wrong. Looking in a mirror also helps if you cannot decide whether your design works or not.

Choice of colour is individual, but tradition does offer some guidelines with which to start. In Japanese design, motifs are symbolic, and so are some colours. Orange-red is a colour for good luck. Children are dressed in this colour whilst they are small – not the traditional western colours of pink for a girl and blue for a boy. It is also the colour worn to a Japanese wedding along with the purity of white. Red and white together signify happiness and celebration. Green is the colour of eternal life shown by evergreens like the pine tree, which never change colour whatever the season. Black depicts mystery and solemnity. Gold is the colour of heaven.

Nature is often the inspiration for colours in Japanese design. Here, maple leaves are pictured in front of the most celebrated view in Japan – Mount Fuji, or Fuji-san as it is known.

Japanese design is influenced by the seasons and it is unusual to find flowers grouped together unless they bloom at the same time. Choose the right colours and shades to match the season.

There are many festivals in Japan, many of which are on odd-numbered dates: 1st January (first of the first month), 3rd March (third of the third month), 5th May, 7th July, 9th September. There are symbols and associated colours to represent each festival.

1st January New Year is represented by the Three Friends of Winter or *Sho-chiku-bai*: plum, pine and bamboo. The plum tree flowers so early in the year that its bare wood is deep pink or white with blossom before there are any leaves. Pine and bamboo are evergreen, and bamboo can be a lovely green-gold colour.

3rd March Girls' Day or Doll Festival is represented by dolls and associated with peach blossom and soft peach tones.

5th May Boys' Day is represented by the purple/blue iris, with its strong sword-like leaf, usually depicted in water; and by the carp for its strength and tenacity, fighting its way up a waterfall.

7th July *Tanabata* celebrates the love story between a Heavenly Weaver and a Cowherd who meet once a year via a bridge of magpies in the sky. The festival is represented by the weaving loom or spindles and is associated with the colours of the night sky and cool watery shades to take away the heat of summer.

9th September Chrysanthemum Festival. The sixteen-petal chrysanthemum is the emblem of the emperor's family. Magnificent flower-heads of red/orange and bright yellow dominate autumn design.

Remember that the background colour of the fabric on which you are going to work has a great bearing on the shades and depth of colour you can use. Do not use a colour just because you like it. Think of the work as a whole subject. In Japanese design, one colour, far removed from the rest of the colour range, is often used sparingly to shock the eye. A surprise attracts the eye and makes the viewer stop and look closer.

Handling flat silk

One of the most important things to consider when handling flat silk is whether your hands are smooth (a love affair with good hand cream benefits you well). If you do snag or ruffle the silk, one tip is to take the strand and run it across your forehead. You should not be wearing make-up, and the natural oils in your skin will smooth out all but the worst cases.

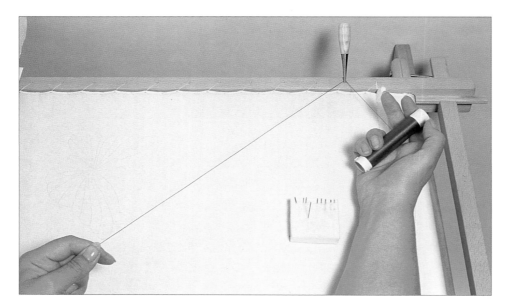

1. Spool the silk off the spool evenly, holding it round the back of the awl as shown, and letting the spool run through your hand. Be sure to run the silk through your fingers and do not be tempted to unwind it, as you are sure to twist it, and the delightful shine of flat silk depends on the thread remaining completely flat.

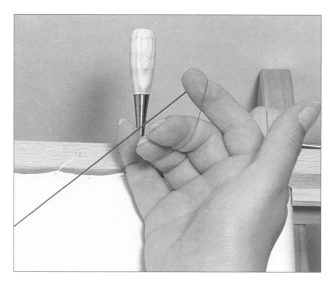

2. Take hold of both strands of the silk thread with your right hand.

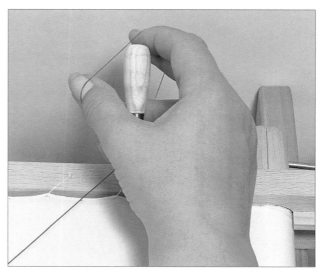

3. Anchor the thread round the awl.

24

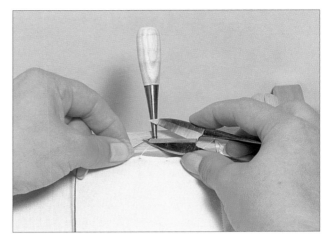

5. Place your needle into the needle felt. Cut the thread off the awl.

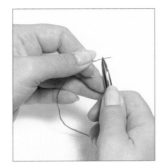

6. Knot the ends of the thread and snip off the tail.

4. Thread up the needle with the two loose ends.

Stroking flat silk

To keep your silk flat, not twisted, and under tension, you need to stroke it with your *teko-bari* (stroking needle.) Before pulling a stitch right down, stroke the silk flat, like a ribbon. Keep the *teko-bari* under the silk until the stitch is pulled right down.

25

Twisting threads

In order to make a 4 into 1 twisted thread, pass the silk thread round the awl twice. If you were making a 2 into 1 thread, you would only pass it round the awl once. If making a thicker thread, pass the thread round the number of times required (i.e. three times for a 6 into 1, etc.)

Sit back from your frame when twisting, as this allows you to be more fluid with your hand movements.

1. Pass your thread around the awl twice and cut to length, remembering to cut through the loop to make four threads of equal length.

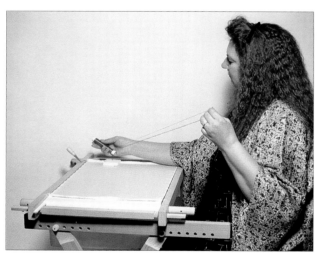

2. Anchor the threads to the awl as for flat silk (see step 3, page 24). Take two of your four threads and pass them round the back of the awl, so that you now have two threads on either side of the awl, separated from one another.

3. Hold the left-hand thread in your mouth. Take the right-hand thread in your left hand, place it on the heel of your right hand and run it up from the base of your right hand to your right finger-tips. This is the undertwist.

Note
Do not let go of the twisted thread. Once it has been twisted, it must be kept taut.

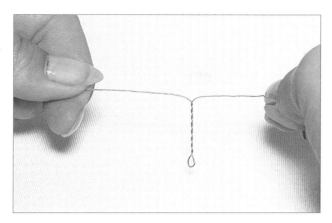

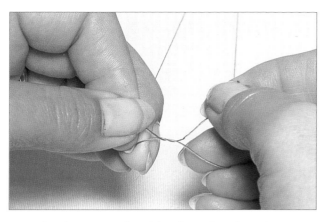

4. To test whether the thread is twisted enough, hold out a portion of the thread and relax it a little. You should get a twist with a loop at the bottom. Put the end of the twisted thread into your mouth and twist the other side of the thread. When tested, it should have the same sized loop.

5. Take the two ends of the thread and tie them to make sure that they are the same length.

6. Run the threads up your left hand as before, to combine the threads. This is the overtwist.

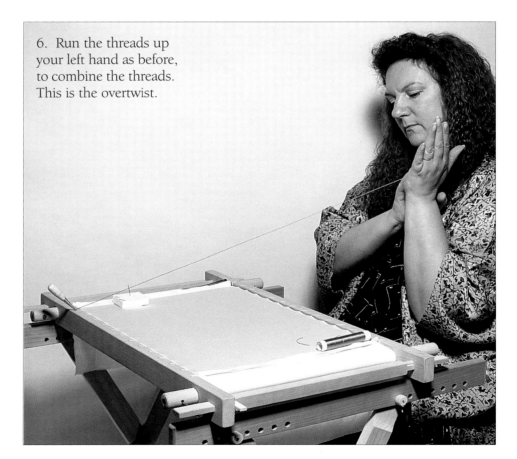

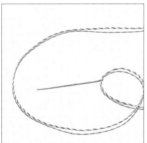

A twisted thread ready to stitch. This type of twist is called a 'z' twist.

Note
Twisting the undertwist up your left hand and the overtwist up your right hand makes an 's' twist.

Handling metallic threads

You should treat metallic threads with great care, winding them on to the *koma* with a gentle rhythm, in a beckoning motion. Stitchable metallic threads (usually no. 1 gold), should be placed into paper for protection, and then one end cut to leave manageable lengths with which to stitch. Lengths should be kept straight, and when working with pairs of threads, always keep them parallel and stop them from twisting up on each other.

Making a half-hitch

1. Take a length of no. 1 gold thread and thread both ends through the eye of the needle.

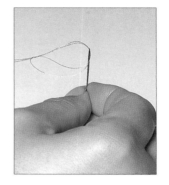

2. Take those two ends back through the loop. Tighten to make a half-hitch. Tie a knot in the two ends and cut off any tails. You are now ready to stitch.

Couching metallic thread

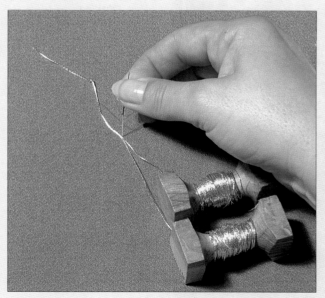

When couching, your metallic threads will be wound on to two *koma*. Take the end from each *koma* and knot them together. Lay the metallic threads on to the surface of your silk. Make a tiny backstitch with fine couching silk. Come up at the start of the design. Couch over the threads at right angles with your couching thread, leaving the tail end free.

Making and using a sinking needle

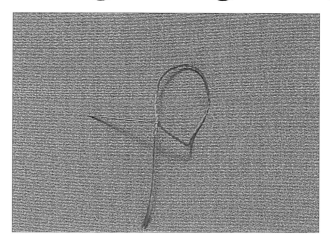

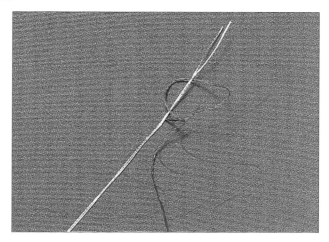

1. Thread a needle with one strand of silk. Anchor the needle in your cotton ends at the edge of your work. Twist each side of the thread on the needle, as you would on the awl, then twist them together. Snip off the end to leave about 10cm (4in). This is a sinking needle. This becomes a tool of your trade, and you keep it until the silk frays, then make a new one.

2. To sink your metallic thread ends, cut the knot off the tail of your metallic threads, then thread the trimmed ends through the loop of the sinking needle. Put the sinking needle through the silk as close to the first couched stitch as possible, without losing the first couching stitch.

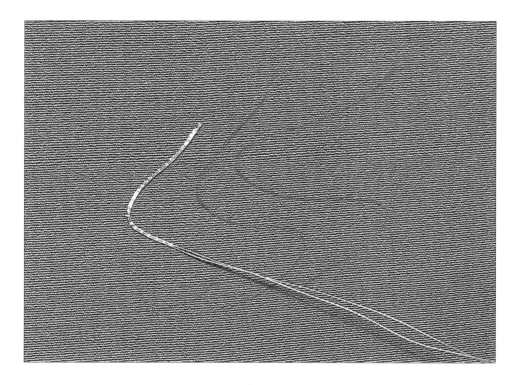

3. Pull the sinking needle down sharply. The loop pulls the ends through to the back of the work.

Winter

Sho-chiku-bai ~ Three Friends of Winter

Plum, pine and bamboo, the 'three friends of winter' in Japanese culture, are also the heralds of spring. Plum (*ume*) blossom on bare wood is the first flower to brave frost and extreme cold, coming out before even the leaves. It is considered fragrant, graceful and feminine.

Pine (*matsu*) is evergreen, and thus beautiful in all weathers. It shows great strength and fortitude, and represents masculinity as well as longevity. The needles grow in pairs, and remain together when they fall, and so are a symbol of fidelity.

Bamboo (*sho*) is the most important of Japanese plants. It is impossible to picture Japan without thinking of bamboo: its myriad uses form part of the basis of everyday life. Bamboo is both pliant and strong, and remains in leaf through the coldest times, and therefore represents flexibility and reliability.

The combination expresses the wish for long life, good fortune, strength and beauty even in the face of adversity.

This design was worked on a natural ivory silk. This makes the choice of thread colours easier, since there is no 'interference' by a background colour. When you begin choosing your own colours, it is advisable to start in this way, before using coloured or patterned backgrounds. The colours chosen here are natural: the *ume* plum really is this colour in flower. For the pine, I chose a strong, masculine green, and for the bamboo a young, vibrant green for the new leaves.

Ume *plum blossom flowers on bare wood in winter, even before the leaves come out.*

Above right: This pine tree in Osaka, Japan, has been clipped to create the distinctive shape used in our design. Bamboo (left) is vital to Japanese life, and symbolises reliability and flexibility.

Sho–chiku–bai — Three Friends of Winter

Design size
18 x 13cm (7 x 5in)

Silk fabric
Natural ivory shioze

Threads
Plum blossom: deep pink, 1025, 2/1 flat
  stamens: no. 1 gold couched with gold silk, 1/2 twist
  plum bough: no. 1 gold half-hitch

Pine tree: deep green, 1067, 4/1 twist
  boughs: no. 1 gold half-hitch
  branches: no. 1 gold couched with gold silk, 1/2 twist
Bamboo: gold green, 1071 or 424, 2/1 flat;
  stalks no. 1 gold
  veins: no. 1 gold couched with gold silk, 1/2 twist

> ### Note
> All the **design sizes** given are from the edges of
> the stitches, top to bottom and then side to side.

Plum blossom

When working with *shioze* silk, bring the needle up to begin in the valley of the fabric. Make sure your needle comes up at a 90° angle to the fabric. Begin working your plum blossom in satin stitch, stitching the petals in the order shown below.

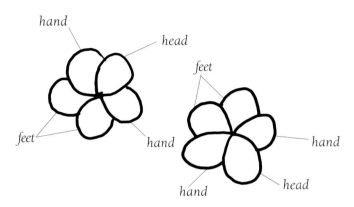

A plum blossom has five petals, and these are stitched in a certain order. First, find the 'head' petal. This is not necessarily at the top of the flower – it is the whole foreground petal, and this is always stitched first. The petals either side of the head are the 'hands', and are stitched next. The final two petals are the 'feet', and the background petal of these two is stitched last.

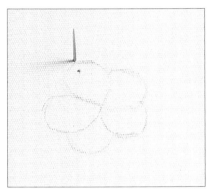

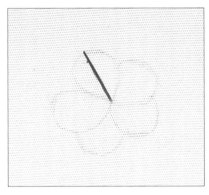

1. Transfer your design (see page 21). Tie a knot in the deep pink thread and cut off the tail. Bring the needle up through the silk and make a tiny back stitch. Do not put the back stitch where you need to stitch your stamen later, as it will be in the way of the needle. Then come up ready to start your first stitch.

2. Stitch the centre line, bringing the needle up through the top of the petal and down through the bottom.

3. Work a line of stitches from left to right and from the top to the bottom of the petal. Then work from the centre, stitching from right to left and from the top to the bottom of the petal, to complete the petal. Fasten off after completing a petal.

Note

It is best to fasten off after completing each petal, as taking the thread across from petal to petal may result in you seeing a dark line showing through your silk fabric when you stand back from your work.

4. Work the 'hands' in the same way, leaving a needle point's space between the petals.

5. Finally work the 'feet' in the same way, finishing with the background petal.

6. To fasten off, part two strands of thread that you have already stitched, with the *teko-bari*. Come up between them, and make two tiny back stitches in the space between the threads. Make sure the stitches are made in a valley of the fabric, to avoid making a bump in the embroidery.

7. Come up again in the same space and snip off the thread.

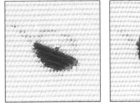

8. Now stitch the buds, beginning in the middle as with the flower petals. Stitch to the edge of a bud, and then fill in the other side. Stitch all the buds in the same way. The branches on which the buds appear will later be stitched in gold, but the flat silk is always finished before beginning on the gold thread.

33

Stamens

The stamens are shown here stitched on to a blank design for clarity. In fact, you will stitch them on top of the deep pink silk of the petals.

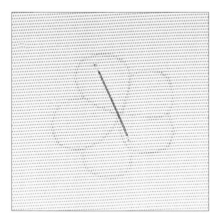

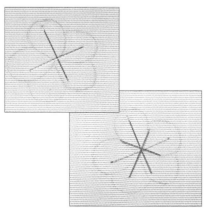

9. First thread your needle with no. 1 gold as shown on page 28. Start with a tiny back stitch as before. Bring the needle up through the centre of the 'head' petal and down through a 'foot' petal, making sure that the thread lies across the centre of the flower.

10. Make another stitch at right angles dividing the flower into four. Make two more stitches to divide the flower into eight and then another four making sixteen. All of these stitches are of random length and as before lie across the centre of the flower.

11. Make a cross stitch to anchor all of these threads to the centre.

Note
When making the cross stitch, pull the threads down a little away from the head petal. This will make the flower look more natural.

12. Then pull and couch each stamen into a curve, curving down from the top stamen.

The finished flower with the gold stamens in place.

Pine tree

The rule in Japanese embroidery is to work the foreground first, so work the whole pine tree first. The tree is shown on its side, as this is the direction in which you will be stitching, working sideways on to the design.

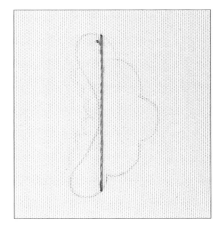

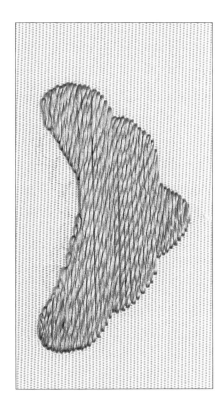

1. As for the flower, put in one tiny back stitch. Then, starting with the widest stitch, bring your needle up though the silk at the top and down through the bottom.

2. Fill in the right-hand side (as you are working) in this way.

3. Fill in the left-hand side in the same way, starting from the longest stitch as before.

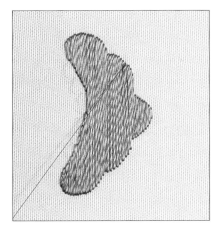

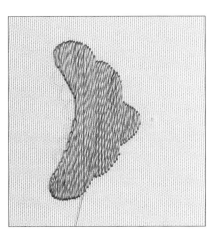

Note
To make a couching thread, anchor your thread round the awl, split it into two strands, then split one of those portions of a strand into two again. Twist together two of the quarters to make one fine thread for couching.

4. Thread a needle with the couching thread and bring the needle up through the silk. Move the thread across the tree. If it shows up, it is in the wrong place, as above.

5. Once the couching thread disappears into the background threads, as above, it is in the right place.

6. Bring the needle down through the fabric. Bring your next stitch up 2.5mm ($^1/_8$in) away from the last stitch and parallel to it. Continue in this way until the grid covers the pine tree.

7. Couch the grid down using the same thread and tiny couching stitches. These stitches should come up and go down through the centre of a background stitch. The couching stitches should be 3mm (just over $^1/_8$in) apart.

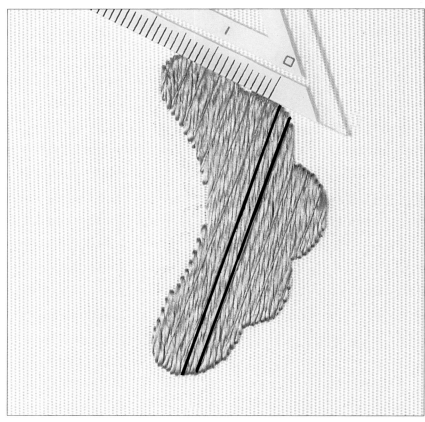

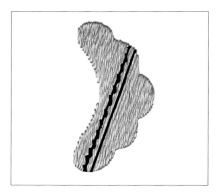

8. Measure the gold branches from the design sheet. Stitch the centre upright first. Using no. 1 gold, stitch the branches starting at the centre and working out.

Note
Check that the branches are equidistant (approx. 4mm/ $^1/_4$in apart) to maintain perfection.

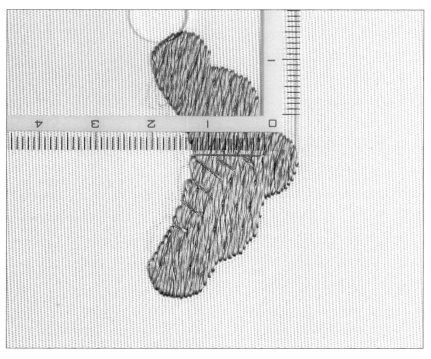

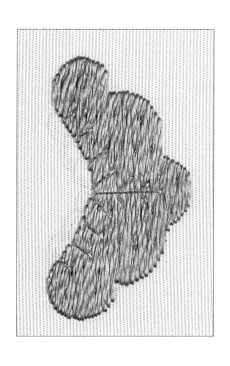

9. Complete the branches on the other side as shown.

10. Couch down the straight branches with gold silk couching thread. The upright should be couched straight. The other branches should be pulled down slightly in the middle to make them curve. One is shown curved here.

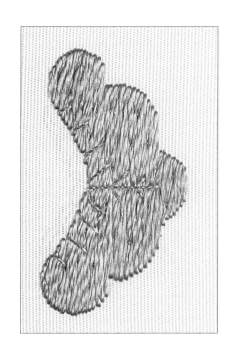

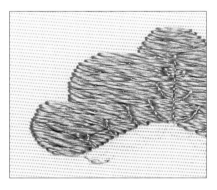

11. Using no. 1 gold thread, stitch the boughs with staggered diagonals. Put in the first stitch...

12. ...then the second goes in slightly diagonal to the first, about a third of the way along and going a third past it, to create a curve.

13. The third stitch starts a third of the way along the second, to complete the curve. Stitch all the boughs of the pine tree in the same way. Staggered diagonals and gold thread are also used to stitch the branches on which the pink buds appear.

Bamboo

Begin with the foreground leaf, i.e. the whole leaf in the centre. Then, as this design is in the centre of the fabric, it will be the next leaf towards you that you stitch next. Remember always to leave a needle point's space in between the leaves.

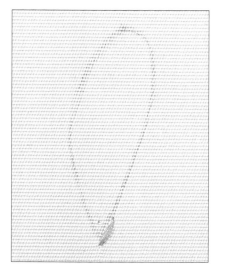 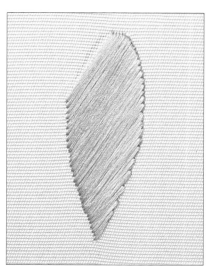 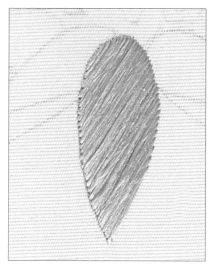

1. Start with the whole foreground leaf, which in this design is in the middle. Put in your first stitch at the correct angle at the point of the leaf.

2. Stitch at the same angle to the top of the leaf.

3. Finish the leaf as shown.

Note

It is best to finish stitching the silk before adding metallic work to your piece, so finish all the leaves before adding their vein lines.

4. Work from the middle leaf towards yourself, then turn the frame around and work towards yourself on the other side. Put in your stitches at the angles shown for each leaf.

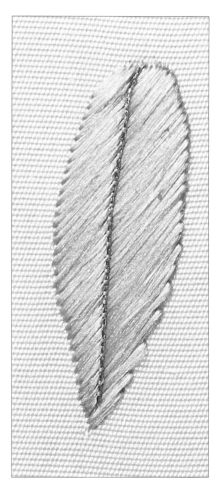

6. Couch the vein line into a curve with gold silk couching thread. Complete all the gold vein lines in the same way.

5. Using no. 1 gold, put in the vein line in the centre of the middle leaf. Do not take the vein right down to the point of the leaf, as this will not look natural.

7. Begin to stitch the bamboo stalks in no. 1 gold, as shown.

8. Finish stitching the gold stalks.

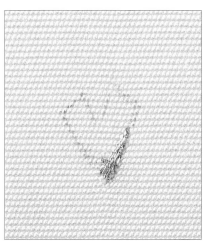

These Three Friends of Winter (Sho-chiku-bai) appear in many design forms. Here is another on which to practise. The two examples show how a different choice of colours can change the appearance of the design: in the one above the buds are white, and in the design opposite the branches are stitched in brown instead of gold. Stitching within the lines you have drawn, instead of going over them, creates Japonica quince blossom (opposite) instead of plum.

Sho-chiku-bai — Three Friends of Winter with White Buds

Design size
16.5 x 16.5cm (6½ x 6½in)

Silk fabric
Natural ivory shioze

Threads
Plum blossom: deep pink, 1025, 2/1 flat
   stamens: no. 1 gold couched with gold silk, 1/2 twist
   buds: white, 1086, 2/1 flat
   plum bough: no. 1 gold half-hitch
Pine trees: deep green, 1067, 4/1 twist
   boughs: no. 1 gold half-hitch
   branches: no. 1 gold couched with gold silk, 1/2 twist
Bamboo: gold green, 1071, 2/1 flat
   veins: no. 1 gold couched with gold silk, 1/2 twist

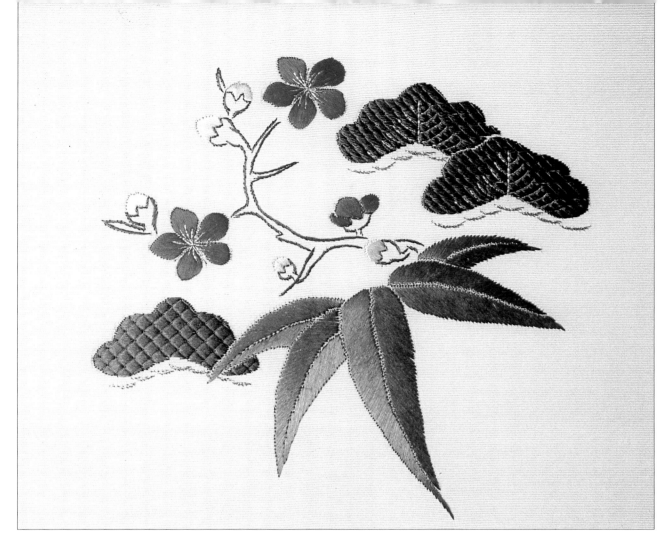

Sho-chiku-bai — Three Friends of Winter with Japonica Quince

Design size
16.5 x 16.5cm (6½ x 6½in)

Silk fabric
Natural ivory shioze

Threads
Quince flower: deep pink, 1025, 2/1 flat
  stamens: no. 1 gold couched with gold silk, 1/2 twist
  buds: pale pink, 1019, 2/1 flat
  quince bough: dark brown, 1074 or 747, 2/1 flat
Pine trees: deep green, 1067, 4/1 twist
  boughs: no. 1 gold half-hitch
  branches: no. 1 gold couched with gold silk, 1/2 twist
Bamboo: green, 424, 2/1 flat
  veins: no. 1 gold couched with gold silk, 1/2 twist

Spring

Cho-cho ~ Butterflies and Falling Petals

The butterfly symbolises rebirth. It is believed to be a fallen petal returning to the bough.

Cherry blossom, the petals of which feature in this design, is a symbol of womanhood. It is also the emblem of the *samurai* (warrior), since each blossom only lives for a single day, and therefore symbolises the shortness of life. The *samurai* was prepared to give up his life for the protection of his master. Cherry blossom is an important flower in Japan, and gives rise to the *O-hanami* or cherry blossom viewing festival, during which Japanese people sit beneath the newly flowering trees and have picnics. It is considered a good meditation to sit and watch a single flower open on a sunny day.

This design combines a celebration of womanhood with a wish for a long and happy life, and for rebirth, to continue the cycle of living into infinity.

I have chosen the spring-like, soft, creamy yellow as a background colour, and light, young shades for the butterflies and petals.

Cho–cho — Butterflies and Falling Petals

Design size
20 x 15cm (8 x 6in)

Silk fabric
Cream shioze

Threads
Bottom butterfly: medium blue purple, 614, 1/1 flat
Bottom small butterfly: medium yellow green, 476, 1/1 flat
Middle butterfly: blue purple, 613, 1/1 flat
Top silk butterfly: yellow green, 474, 1/1 flat
Top butterfly: 1 pair no. 1 gold couched with gold silk
body padding: butter yellow, 318, 2/1 flat
body: no. 1 gold half-hitch
antennae: one pair no. 1 gold couched with gold silk
Petals: orange, 202 and 204, 1/1 flat

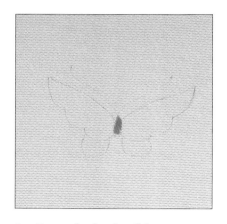 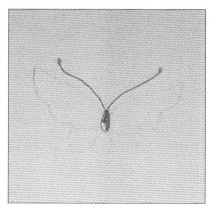 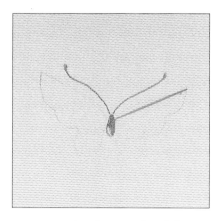

1. Cover the body of the butterfly with silk padding stitches. These are simply satin stitches that will give the body a raised appearance.

2. Stitch over the padding stitches in the opposite direction with no. 1 gold thread, and lay and couch the antennae, as shown on page 28. Sink the ends of the gold thread as shown on page 29.

3. Put in the first stitch of the foreground wing. The longest stitch comes first, as shown. This gives you the correct angle for the rest of the stitches.

4. Fill in both the foreground wings, stitching in the direction shown above. Then fill in the background wings as shown. Stitch all the main butterflies in the same way as in steps 1–4.

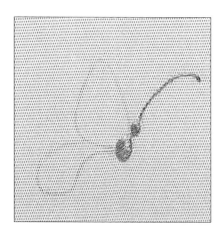

5. Repeat steps 1–2 on the gold outlined butterfly.

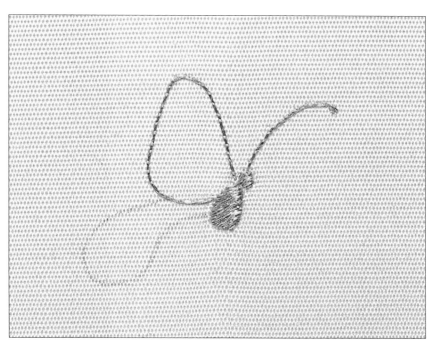

6. Couch and sink the top wing with gold couching silk.

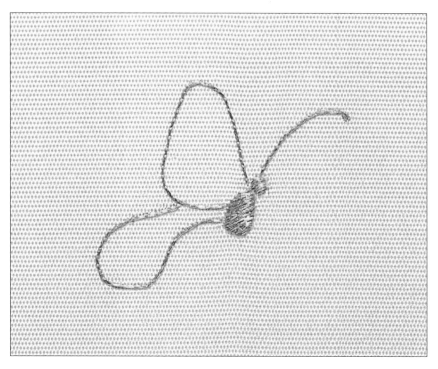

7. Couch and sink the bottom wing.

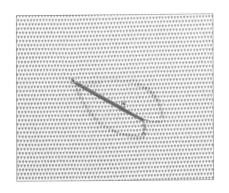

8. Stitch the centre line of the first flat falling petal.

9. Finish stitching the first petal. Stitch all the flat petals in the same way.

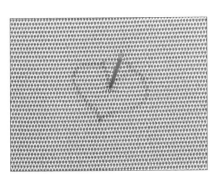

10. Stitch the foreground part of the curled petal.

11. Stitch the rest of the curled petal in the same direction. Stitch all the curled petals in the same way.

Stitching a large butterfly is not very different to stitching a small one, providing it is worked in sections. The body of this one has cotton padding stitches as well as silk, to give a more rounded look. The play of light on the silk threads of the wings will make the butterfly look more three-dimensional, and there is no 'clever' shading needed.

Cho-cho — Single Butterfly

Design size
13 x 16.5cm (5 x 6½in)

Silk fabric
Black shioze

Threads
Butterfly's top wings: wood rose, 697, 2/1 flat
Bottom wings: wood rose, 694, 2/1 flat
Body: under layer padding: 5/1 cotton;
silk padding: golden cream, 902, 2/1 flat;
top layer: no. 1 gold half-hitch
Antennae: one pair no. 4 gold couched with gold silk

Summer

Tsubaki ~ Camellia in Water

The camellia is an interesting flower, as instead of shedding individual petals, it drops the whole flower. The *samurai* were said to be wary of the camellia, as it loses its whole head – but it can also be said to retain its beauty even when fallen. The saying goes that 'the camellia will always prosper in frost and snow'.

Here the water swirls to take away the heat of the summer for all who look upon it. As these designs would originally have been stitched on to kimono, it would have been the onlooker who benefited, not the wearer. Water and waves represent repetitive movement: the tides turn every day and water flows continuously; waves wash on to the shore into infinity. This design therefore symbolises the wish for long life.

The Japanese artist is taught that even when painting a dot in the eye of a tiger, he or she must first feel the feline, savage, cruel nature of the creature. If painting a storm, he or she must at that very moment feel the force of the wind and the power of the rain. So feel the coolness of the water as it swirls around your design, or the lightness and fragility of a butterfly in flight. Add strength, character and feeling to your work and keep telling the stories in your stitches.

Camellia flowering in Tokyo

A fallen camellia in Kenrokuen Garden, Kanazawa, Japan.

48

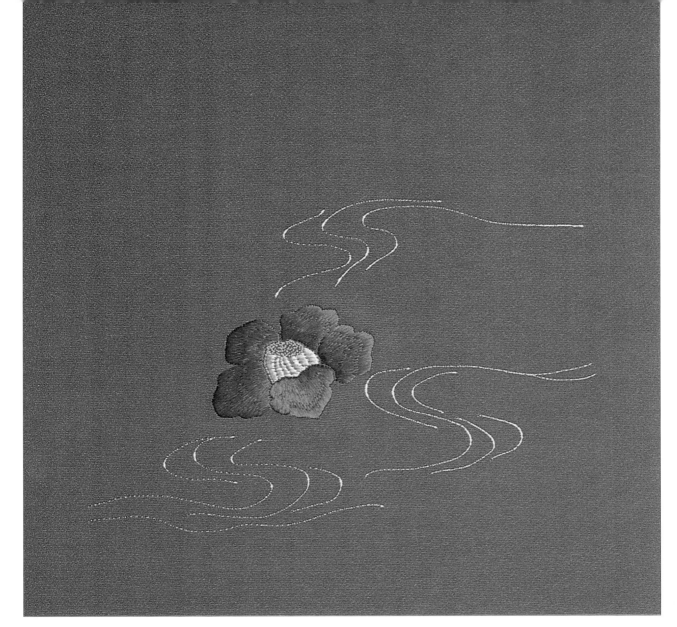

Tsubaki — Camellia in Water

Design size
17.5 x 25.5cm (7 x 10in)

Silk fabric
Blue kimono silk

Threads
Camellia: plum, 687, first line 3/1 flat; second line 1.5
flat, third and fourth line 1 flat

Flower centre: butter yellow, 314, 1 flat

Detail: one pair no. 1 gold couched with gold silk

Stamen: knots, 314, 2/1 's' twist

Water: one pair no. 4 silver couched with white silk

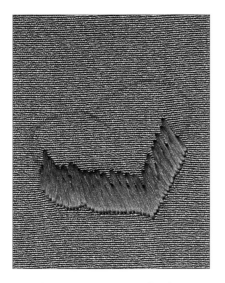 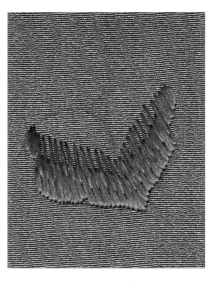 

1. The camellia is stitched in long and short stitches. Start off in the usual way. Put in the first line of stitches: one long followed by one short.

2. Put in the second line of one long, one short stitches.

3. Work the whole petal in the same way. You may need three or four rows of stitches to complete it.

4. Lay the first yellow silk stitch across the centre of the flower.

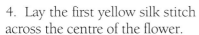

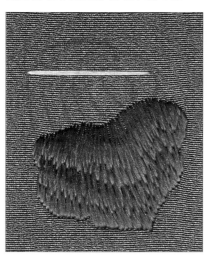

5. Stitch across the whole centre of the flower in the same way. Then lay a metallic gold thread going in the opposite direction towards the flower's centre. Lay five more gold threads in the same way, and couch them all into a curves.

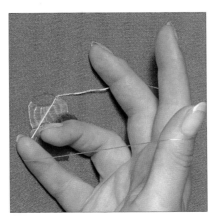

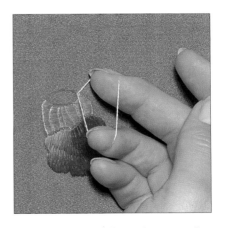

6. Now you need to make the knots at the flower's centre. Twist your thread on the awl, the opposite way to a 'z' twist. Twist the undertwist up your left hand and the overtwist up your right hand, to make an 's' twist (see page 27). Thread your needle and start with a tiny backstitch as usual.

7. Pull the needle down with your left hand, holding on to the wider loop with your right hand, and the small loop down against the fabric. This ensures a nice, even knot.

8. Continue pulling down with your left hand, ensuring that the knot is made on the fabric, not above it.

10. Lay a pair of no. 4 silver threads (using your *koma* as on page 28) and couch them in place using white couching thread. Lay and couch the other water swirls. Sink the metallic threads as shown on page 29.

9. Fill the centre of the flower with knots in the same way. Fill in all the petals from the centre out, as shown.

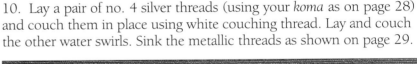

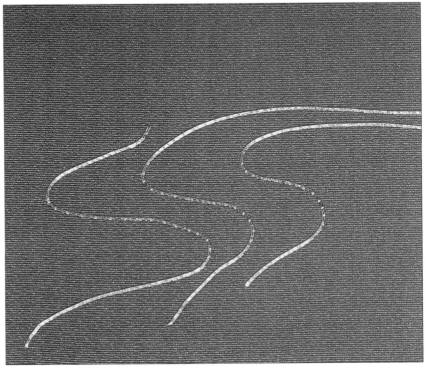

The iris, which inspired the design opposite, is the symbol for the Boys' Day festival in Japan. The leaf is thought to resemble the blade of a sword, and the flower is usually featured in water, often with a carp, to represent strength, a warrior spirit and other 'manly' qualities.

Kakitsubata — Iris

Design size
17.5 x 17.5cm (7 x 7in)

Silk fabric
Blue kimono silk

Threads
Iris: bright blue, 527
centre petals: 2/1 flat
outer petals 4/1 twist
Leaves: green, 408, 2/1 flat
Water: one pair no. 4 silver couched
in white silk

Autumn

Momiji ~ Maple

Autumn maple leaves suggest the approaching close of the year. Dressing in their final gorgeous hues, they are associated with brilliant, warm and resplendent colours. Maples can also be used in spring designs, in shades of young green. When the maple leaf is used alone in a design, it is said to suggest loneliness.

Maple leaf viewing is another time for gazing up into the trees, like the cherry blossom festival. Trees are lit up at night, especially in public gardens or temple grounds, for people to walk beneath and see breathtaking collections of colours. With carpets of fallen leaves beneath the trees, they cause many camera shutters to click in the hope of obtaining a prize-winning picture.

This design, being on black, allows the freedom to choose from any of the glorious, bright shades of autumn. Softer shades can be added, as this ensures that the brighter ones stand out and attract the eye, more than if you assault your audience with too much colour. Remember, 'less is more'! The black background works like the night sky, so that the play of colour is concentrated in the leaves, which look lit up.

Maple leaves cause many a click of camera shutters, especially where these are seen here, near Mount Fuji.

54

Momiji — Maple

Design size
20 x 25.5cm (8 x 10in)

Silk fabric
Black shioze

Threads
All silk leaves are 4/1 twist
Gold leaves: 1 pair no. 1 gold couched with gold silk
Pair of leaves in top left hand corner: red/orange – 117
Group of three on right: top, golden-rod, 336

middle, apricot, 226
bottom, orange brown, 726
Bottom group of four: foreground leaf: orange, 202
middle left, red/orange, 113
middle right, red/orange, 115

1. Starting with the fattest side of the fattest finger of the foreground leaf, put in the first stitch as shown.

2. Continue up one side of the first finger, as shown.

3. Complete the second side of the first finger as shown. Begin the second finger of the leaf in the same way, fattest side first.

4. Continue in the same way until the whole leaf is stitched. Stitch all the silk leaves in the same way.

5. Couch the edge of the gold outline leaf, using your *koma* as shown on page 28 and working in a clockwise direction. Sink the metallic threads.

6. Couch and sink the veins in the same way.

Ginkgo trees line some streets in Japan, and Osaka Prefecture has taken the tree as its symbol. It is considered a venerable tree, known to live for a long time, indeed I have seen one that is believed to have lived for 1,600 years. It therefore symbolises the wish for longevity, and it is usually stitched in the young green of spring or the golden yellow of autumn.

Ginkgo

Design size
23 x 15cm (9 x 6in)

Silk fabric
Orange shusu

Thread
1 pair no. 1 gold couched with gold silk

Finishing off

If your work doesn't look quite right, never be afraid to do a little reverse stitching (taking out). The one little bit you decide to leave as you 'won't notice it' will be the one piece your eye goes to each time you look at that embroidery. So aim for perfection in all that you do, but do not become so obsessed with it that you lose the true enjoyment – that of creating a work of beauty with needle and thread.

Now we have reached the finale, and it is time to finish off your work, ready for framing. You need to be especially careful at this stage, as you could ruin a wonderful embroidery if you tackle this part in haste.

Even now I worry about combining water, glue and silk. If you steam your work too much, it could become too wet, and will dry with water marks. If the kettle spits, or if you do, it will leave a mark. This is why, when viewing another embroiderer's work, we cover our mouths and keep speaking to a minimum. If your glue goes over your stitching line, it will leave a mark.

Yes, I *do* mean to frighten you, because if you take care now, there will be no regrets later!

When viewing another embroiderer's work, you should cover your mouth and speak as little as possible, to avoid ruining months of hard work. Your own work should be treated with the same respect.

Snipping off threads and pounding

This is a time for tidying up. Hopefully your embroidery is neat on the reverse, as any excess thread can snag your silk when stitching. Long ends will need to be cut ready for gluing.

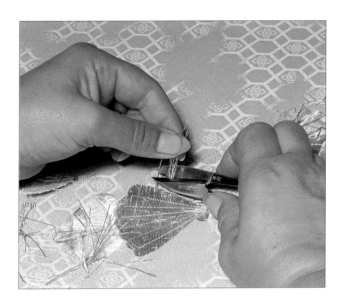

1. Turn your work over on to the reverse side (this is the only time you will see the reverse of your embroidery). Snip off all loose ends, using traditional Japanese scissors. Leave roughly 1cm (½in) of thread. I always collect the ends in a special snippings pot.

2. Take a lint-free silk cushion filled with collected snippings, or anything else dust and lint-free. Pound your work on the reverse side, very vigorously, to get rid of the dust or tiny snippings of thread. This will make your work shine.

Gluing

Traditionally, glue is applied with the fingertips, but I find it easier to put on the glue with a chisel-ended bristle brush. I check that not too much has been applied with my fingertips.

1. Place a small amount of glue in the palm of your hand.

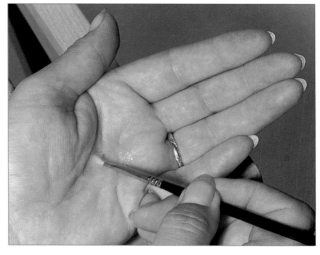

2. Rub it around with a brush to make a smooth paste. The warmth of your hand melts the glue.

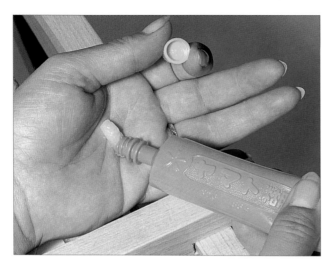

3. Use the brush to apply glue to the stitched area only. Do not go over the edges of the stitched area. Brush in the direction of the stitch.

4. Smooth with your finger to make sure the glue is not overloaded, or it will go through to the right side of the work.

Steaming

Put the work right-side up and put a full kettle under your work station, on a low stool, on a tray. Keep the kettle boiling for at least three minutes. This revitalises your silk, sets the threads and gets rid of any grime.

Note

The minimum distance between the top of the kettle and your embroidery should be approximately 30cm (12in). If you have a long embroidery, you may need to move the kettle occasionally to ensure an even steam over the whole piece.

Pressing

Place a piece of finishing paper (I use baking parchment) on top of your embroidery. Switch your iron to its silk setting, then stroke it very lightly over the paper. Put your other hand under the embroidery to stop the iron from pressing too hard, or the heat becoming too much for your work. If it burns the hand, it burns the silk. Do not press down on the fabric as you do this. Remove the paper and leave the work to dry naturally overnight – never leave it near a source of heat.

Blocking

I always mount my work over card and wadding. Blocking gives a firm base on which to have your work framed. I do not trust a framer to do this for me!

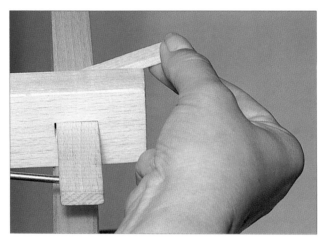

1. Remove the wooden wedges from the frame to release the tension.

2. Release your work from the frame by snipping around the lacing.

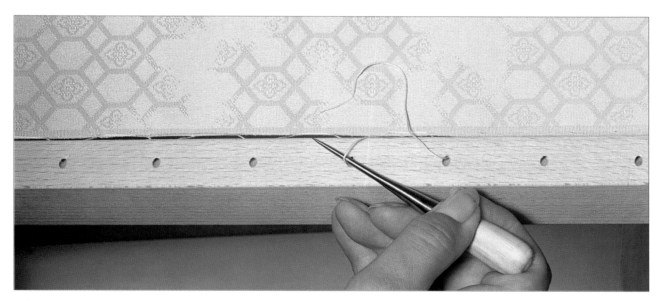

3. Remove the threads gently using the awl.

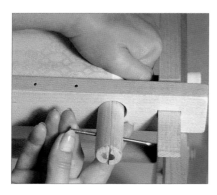

4. Take the pressure off with your other hand, so that you can take out the nails.

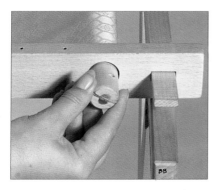

5. Unwind the rollers so that you can lift the embroidery off the frame.

6. Put the embroidery face down on a clean cloth on your lap. Take a piece of museum-quality conservation grade card the size of the finished embroidery. Take a piece of silk wadding 2.5cm (1in) larger all the way round than your embroidery. Wrap the wadding around the card.

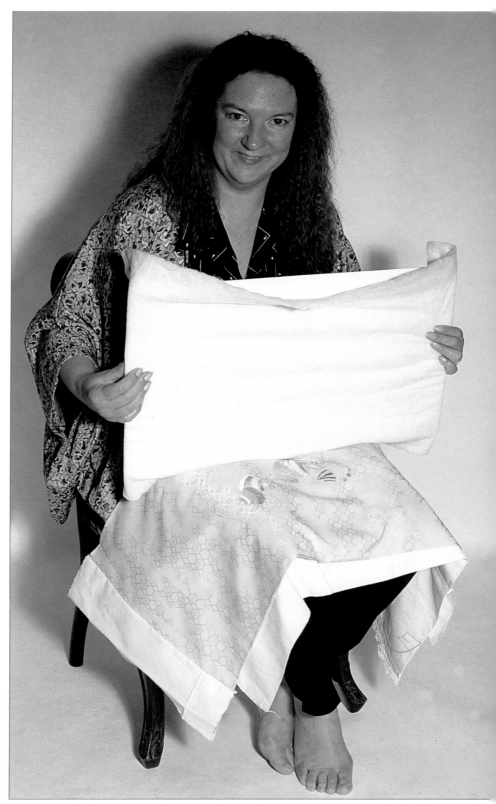

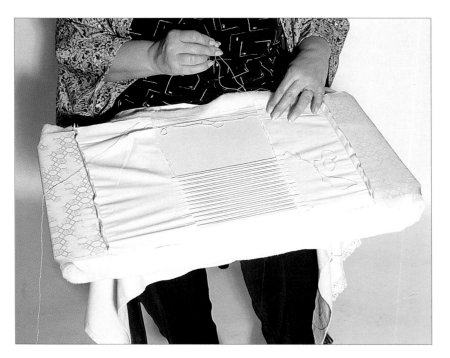

8. Pull each thread of the lacing tight, making sure it is even. Place a finger on each tightened thread to hold the tension while you pull the next thread. Tighten all up one side, then up the other, and repeat each side twice.

7. Wrap the embroidery on top of the wadding around the card. Join the top and bottom of the cotton ends by loosely threading them together using crochet thread and a lacing needle, from the outside edges to the centre. When you reach the centre, go back to the beginning and tie off with a double back stitch. Then begin from the other side and work in to the centre again as shown.

9. Pull the last two threads tight and tie a double knot to pull the centre of your embroidery together.

10. Mitre the corners of the wadding and tuck the wadding in between the lacing and the back of the board.

66

11. Tuck in the selvedge edges at the back of the embroidery. Next you need to lace up the embroidery horizontally, stitching through the front selvedge.

12. Lace up the embroidery horizontally. Start from the sides and work in to the centre as before. Check the front as you go along to make sure the tension is even.

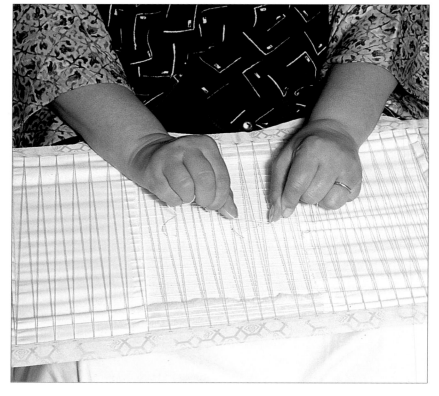

13. Tighten and tie off as before, but not quite as tightly, so that the front looks smooth, with no wrinkles.

Kaigara-nami ~ Sea Wave

The background fabric used here carries the design known as *kikko*, or tortoiseshell. It is the symbol of the turtle, which is very long-lived, but is sometimes considered too ugly to appear in its entirety, so it is represented by the pattern on its shell. This pattern represents the wish for a long life, and, if featured with a crane, a happy one.

Here I have added shells, which are a sign of fidelity, as they break into a pair that make a heavenly match; and a wave, the symbol of the continuity of life, to represent constancy. Whatever happens, the tide will turn each day and the waves will crash on to the beach. The combination expresses the wish for a long and happy marriage. Brides take a game called 'the shell game' into their marriage, to wish for fidelity, as only the two halves of the same shell will match. The game is carried in a Wedding Shell box.

When choosing the colours for this design, I considered the play of light on a changing wave and added unusual metallic threads to try to achieve the look and feel of seashells, which shine differently when viewed from different angles.

This is also another cool design for a summer occasion.

Kaigara-nami — Sea Wave

Design size
28 x 18cm (11 x 7in)

Silk fabric
Green kikko design kimono silk

Threads
Top shell: purple, 1031, 2/1 flat + stitchable metallic
Next shell: green, 1071, 2/1 flat + stitchable metallic
Scallop shell: soft purple, 1028, 2/1 flat; shading: purple, 1027, 1/1 flat
Next shell: stone, 1083, 2/1 flat + stitchable metallic; beige, 1082, 2/1 flat; cream, 1078, 2/1 flat
Bottom shell: shell pink, 1023, 2/1 flat + stitchable metallic; pale pink, 1022, 2/1 flat
Metallic shell: stitchable metallic
Wave: 1 pair no. 3 twisted gold couched with gold silk
Detail: No. 1 gold half-hitch

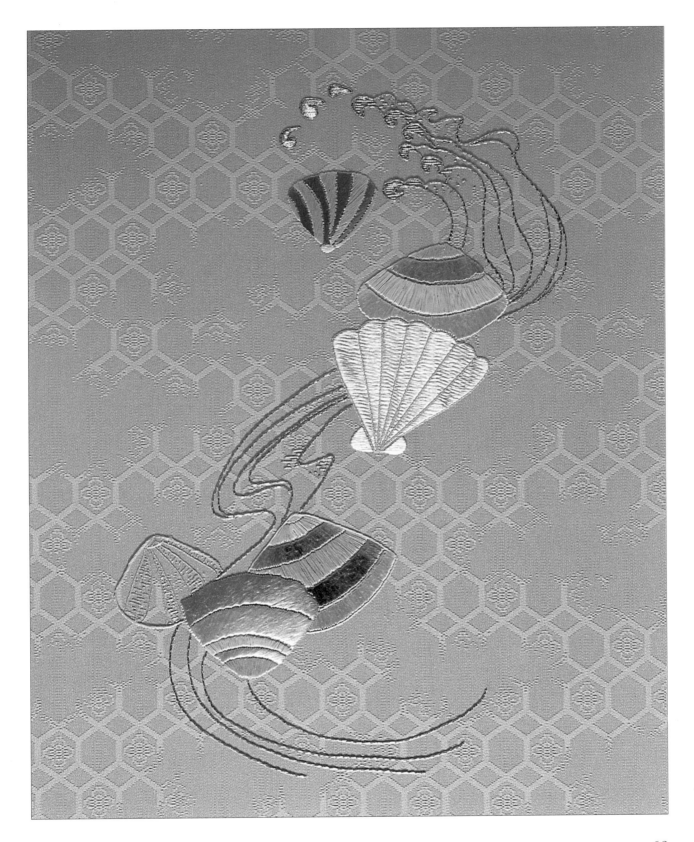

Patterns

Sho–chiku–bai — Three Friends of Winter
This pattern is reproduced full size.

Sho-chiku-bai — Three Friends of Winter with White Buds or Three Friends of Winter with Japonica Quince

This pattern is reproduced full size.

Note

This one pattern is used for the two designs on pages 40 and 41. To achieve the smaller petals of quince blossom, simply stitch inside the drawn lines instead of over them.

Cho-cho — Butterflies and Falling Petals
This pattern is reproduced full size.

72

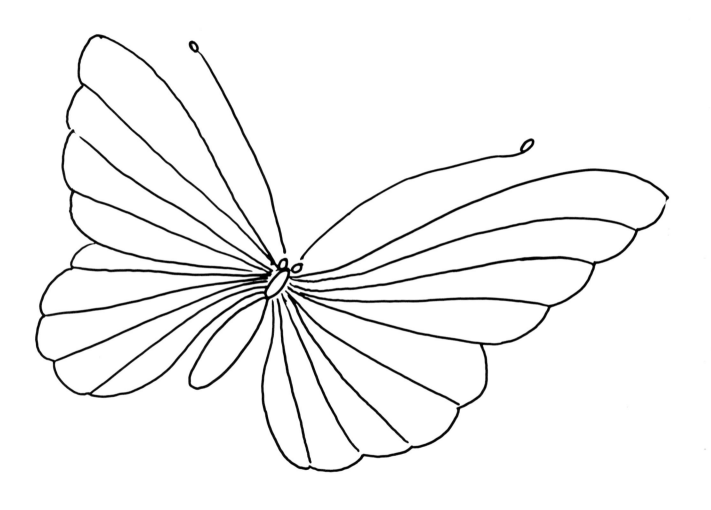

Cho-cho – Single Butterfly
This pattern is reproduced full size.

Tsubaki — Camellia in Water

This pattern has been reduced to fit the page. In
order to reproduce it full size, enlarge it by 133% on
a photocopier.

74

Kakitsubata — Iris
This pattern is reproduced full size.

Momiji — Maple

This pattern has been reduced to fit the page. In order to
reproduce it full size, enlarge it by 133% on a
photocopier.

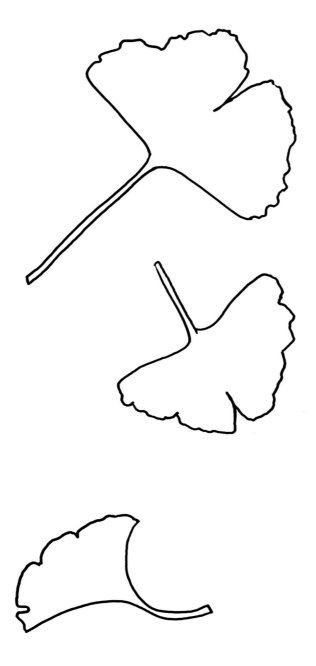

Ginkgo

This pattern has been reduced to fit the page. In order to reproduce it full size, enlarge it by 133% on a photocopier.

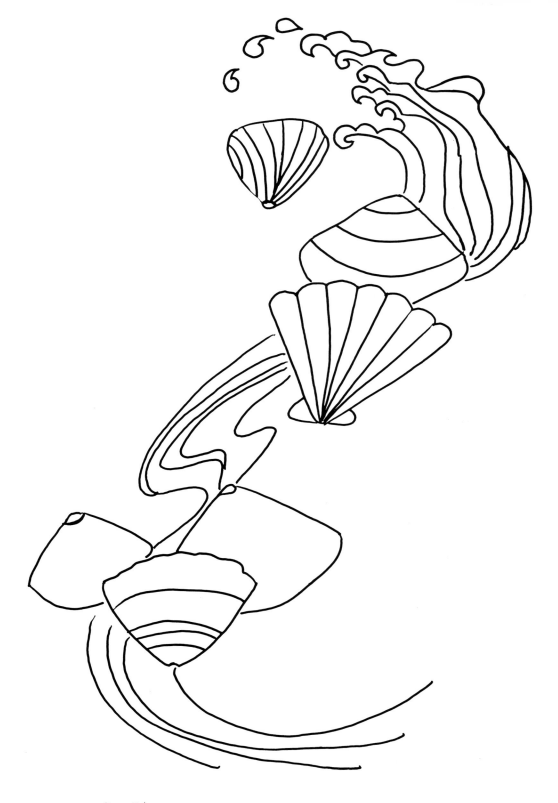

Kaigara-nami — Sea Wave

This pattern has been reduced to fit the page. In order to reproduce it full size, enlarge it by 133% on a photocopier.

About the author

Julia D. Gray's passion for traditional Japanese embroidery was kindled by her interest in Art Nouveau (which was influenced by Japanese design) and further fuelled by the Great Japan Exhibition in London in 1981. She has studied for nine years with Kurenai-kai, graduating at their centre in Atlanta, Georgia, USA in 1995.

Julia researches thoroughly, travelling extensively in Japan to study embroidery and allied traditional crafts including *sumi-e* (ink painting), *yuzen* (silk painting), *shibori* (dyeing) and *katazome* (stencilling). She gives illustrated talks showing her collection of Japanese antique textiles and artefacts and demonstrates at exhibitions throughout Britain.

When not working, Julia enjoys photography, gardening and running her smallholding, all of which bring her close to nature – the inspiration for her work.

Index